wandering in puzzle boxes

Richard H. Fox

ISBN: 978-0-9908413-7-1

Printed in the United States of America

Cover Design: Lea C. Deschenes, Damfino Press, LLC
Front Cover Photo: Mark William Rabiner, *Orpheus* by Cristoforo Stati at the MET
Cover Background Image: xOneca. "Handmade dense labyrinth"
Back Cover Photo: Dan Fox

Also by Richard H. Fox:
Time Bomb

Big Table Publishing Company
Boston, MA
www.bigtablepublishing.com

ACKNOWLEDGMENTS

Grateful acknowledgment is made to the following publications in which these poems appeared or are forthcoming, some in an earlier form:

About Place Journal – "Wind In Pines"
Boston Literary Magazine – "fil de téléphone" and "The other side"
Dămfino – "The Trial Survey"
Ealain – "Anaphora for Ann"
Incessant Pipe – "Summer in St. Louis"
Poetry Quarterly – "Toni tutors townies", "Tefillah echad", "To Katrina, wherever you are, xoxoxo" and "Fifteen years cutting fish in the market, only once…"
Radius – "it was one of us"
Soul-Lit – "Casualty and Medic reconnect on Facebook", "Cpl Jim on his furlough Thanksgiving 1942 - BROWN PHOTO SERVICE, Minneapolis, Minn. DEC 11 1942", "My infusion nurse smiles as she releases the clamp on my pic line and invites Cisplatin in", "Reincarnation at the tag sale", "Rosh Hashanah 5775 – Yom Sheni", "The Scroll of Jeru " and "Unreasonable"
Vietnam War Poetry – "Casualty and Medic reconnect on Facebook"

Special thanks to my wife & best friend Ann, don't know who I'd be without you. Sons Dan & Adam, you make me proud every day. Mom, I must have been fun to raise. My extended family, I am embraced by your love and support.

Heartfelt gratitude to Robin Stratton—for being a light and believing in me. Jane Ellen Ibur—my sister in poetry, wielder of truth and heeded attitude adjustor. Wayne-Daniel Berard—deep-souled Achi, diviner of spirit and wisdom. Dămfino Press, LLC—insightful and skillful editing. John Hodgen & Joe Pacheco—fonts of grace and guidance.

These poems were born in community. Appreciation for my writing groups:

Worcester—Southgate Workshop and Poetry Happens Workshop
Sanibel—Group 3 and Poetry Alliance
ADK/Northampton/St. Pete—Nerissa Nields' Writing It Up In The Garden retreats

Table of Contents

Three

Epilogue

About the Author

In memory of
Melvin Fox
William Gordon Merritt

Hope the greens are breaking true.

Tefillah echad

chant sacred words
        cradle syllables in a sphere of air over tongue
Dad is dying
        doesn't know my kiss
chant slowly
        all tones steps, toe to heel
he has lived more than ninety years
        children, grandchildren, great-grandchildren

every breath saturates my lungs
        seeps out for a full blessing
longer silence between ears' throbbing
        seek their harmony fluttering in chest
Dad's image rests on the back of shut eyelids
        a slideshow of snaps timed to pulse

scan the topography of prayer, savor each utterance
        in dim shadows, light slithers up the spine
the floor i sit on extends to dirt
        body not beheld as separate

i am grateful for every year of Dad's life
        thanks offered as i plunge
into flashes of yearning, grace
        surrender to what was what is what will be
pursuing favors not for myself rather
        mercy for strangers

we are but one another's guests
        spirits wandering in puzzle boxes
hungering to stay and to return

"I was not looking for my dreams to interpret my life, but rather for my life to interpret my dreams."
~ Susan Sontag

"We have to dare to be ourselves, however frightening or strange that self may prove to be."
~ May Sarton

Dance of the wily quail

beer garden, French Quarter, *Montréal*:
      cousin Léon grins, pours Brador.
      as I gulp bottle three, the table spins.
Brador makes malt liquor seem like milk.

we have a laugh, stroll ancient streets.
      at a club open to the sidewalk, a folksinger
      belts out francophone lyrics over a dreadnought.
I sidle to the bar while Léon takes a pee.

sipping a draught, I grab the stool next to a humming man.
      he looks up and smiles, I look down and see
      hash sprinkled over tobacco on Zig-Zag papers.
he doesn't chuckle at *mon Français*, hands me lit *le shit*.

a question is asked, I know the answer but not what he said:
      a story streams out of me, he shakes his hair.
      I don't remember what the words I spoke mean—
mais ils sont plutôt véritable.

Léon taps my shoulder, beckons with his hand.
      I slap palms with the man, he slips a *kif* in my pocket.
      we amble through an alley, up a crooked street to
a brick-floored arena fronted by a covered bandstand.

Léon hops onto the stage, tunes his SG and Strat:
      bandmates jab rapid French laced with vapid slang—
      the drum reads *Le 14 Juillet*, they all wear beards—
Four French Canadians, one Latvian-Jewish Canadian.

drummer counts: they kick off "Aqualung", glide into "Plynth"—
      Léon doing his very best Jeff Beck.
      three-songs-and-two-Molsons later, I'm wet, *il pleut*.
the crowd runs for the roofed market, *je danse*.

my Chuck Taylor high-tops squeak as feet skip brick.
  I flip my bottle, spin, face to the sky—
    arms reach for clouds, puddles splash jeans.
laughter applauds a silly American, the band plays on.

Two truths and one lie

I.

I'm seventeen in 1970 and have stumbled into a date with a girl who is settling for me. My buddy Joseppi offers to chauffeur. We scheme, decide on Whalom Park as our destination. The Roller Coaster, Whip, House of Horrors… centrifugal force and fear molds bodies together. An arm around a shoulder becomes comfort. Prophetic thinking but not the prophesy. The girl & I spin–bump–bang heads. Squealing–laughing–blushing, we seek solid ground–snacks–games of skill.

The carnies see an easy mark and know what to say to a boy with a girl on his arm. The first game is Pool Shark. A billiards ball sits in a circle with a second ball a foot away. The goal is to knock the first ball out of the circle and replace it with the second using a bowed cue. I take a breath and strike the ball with a twist. My ball kisses the circle ball and stops within the mark. Carny One sneers and hands me a twelve inch teddy bear, pink–my date's choice. Feeling that I'm playing with house money, I approach the Knock-'em Sock-'em Dolls. To win, I must disengage a doll from its swivel. The girl smiles at me and I flip a ball as hard as I can. The ball hits between the feet of a doll and the doll slaps up and off. Growl from Carny Two. We are boosted to a twenty-four inch bear.

Joseppi, assuming that I have peaked, suggests it's time to think about hitting Pinecroft Dairy for banana splits, but she winks at me and the Burst-A-Ballon dart game is steps away. Paying more attention to the girl than the target, I spear my dart in the underside of a balloon and it pops. Carny Three grits his teeth, mumbles under his breath, and replaces our bear with a thirty-six incher wearing ruffles and a bonnet. Before I can stroll to the next booth, Joseppi herds us to the car.

At her home, there is a good night kiss but the girl insists I keep the bear. She goes in her front door. I sit the bear on the porch rocking chair.

II.

The Saturday before Thanksgiving 1976, I join the folks of Jefferson City, Missouri at the Annual Turkey Shoot. $20 for five shots, all proceeds benefit the VFW. The birds peck at cracked corn in a log corral tall enough to conceal them unless they pick up their crowns.

I put my money down like every man but have no firearm. Georgie, eldest son of the family who owns the grocery store/butchery, walks by beaming. In his hand, a headless turkey hangs by its neck. Seeing I'm empty handed, he lends me his .287 Weatherby and gives me five cartridges. Always enjoy Georgie. When I visit his market, he goes out back and table saws a bag of marrow bones for my dog.

Today, he slaps me on the back and wishes me luck. I lay on a mat and sight the rifle. Georgie calls *Gobble-gobble-gobble* and a head appears. I don't know whether to try to hit the head because I'd likely miss or try to miss and probably pop it off at the neck. I aim, shoot, and miss high. The men clap and stomp their feet. I decide to sight on the log and squeeze off two rounds. A splinter strikes a bird and I'm awash in catcalls. Georgie gets down next to me and whispers *relax and exhale.* His bird drips blood on my sleeve.

I fire my last bullets. The fourth imbeds in the log but the fifth debeaks a bird. The crowd yells *Yee-hawwww.* I stand up and watch the injured turkey run in circles. Georgie's Dad, who runs the shoot, comes over and claps me on the shoulder. "Good try city boy, but you gotta knock the head off. If no one gets that bird today, we'll butcher him in the store. You want me to phone you so you can buy him?" Georgie nods at me and I nod at his Dad. The next shooter takes my bird's head off with his first shot.

III.

One morning in 1984, I'm traveling west on Cambridge Street from Brosnihan Square. There's a low railroad bridge and the street is graded with a serious dip to allow clearance. In a storm, that patch of road floods enough to float cars. But it's dry that day as I drive under the bridge and ratchet up the radio volume for The Grateful Dead's "Box Of Rain." As I clear the overpass, my eyes drift to the rear-view mirror just in time to see an eighty-thousand-pound freight car derail, roll off the bridge, and occupy the space I'd just vacated. A few months later, our second son is born.

1968
~for Israel Horovitz

chins dip to concealed textbooks–
highlighters slide out of sleeves.
you mount the podium, a hawk's gaze
apprises the house, then a bellow–
Will you strike this school?

with the synchrony of a crack platoon,
every eye sights on you.
texts thump into book bags–
highlighters seek coat pockets–
whispers shatter stillness

though noise in chapel is an offense.
crew cuts stare at one other,
glare at you, the guest speaker
attacking the war in Vietnam, racism,
the military-industrial complex

I am a boy with too-long sideburns,
subject of student experiments:
could I be squeezed into a locker?
how many anti-war flyers fit in my mouth?
could I be spun until I puked?

Will you strike this school?
you throw a chair across the stage.
students charge the exits–
you aim the final volley
Lottery numbers will wake you!

I applaud from the center aisle.
the one student left
in the house–
absolved.

Fifteen years cutting fish in the market, only once...

the Wüsthof fillet knife slips off eel skin
melts into my thumb   a painless slit
I slide the blade out   see the white of bone
stare at the eel on my butcher block
a greasy gray garden hose leaking oil

Nonnina Nunno   (I always put up her fish)
peers through the glass case
taps on a pane as my thumb begins to bleed
I yank it away from Nonnina's eel
she calls *capo uomo, accidenti*

to Wimpy   Maine fisherman   counter kingpin
he limps over   grips my thumb in his left hand
pops a raw scallop in his mouth with his right
drags me by the digit to the utility sink
turns hot water full bore   rinses   squeezes

blood trawls down my hand onto my arm
Wimpy scalds off gore under the tap
presses a white rag to the wound
eases a box of Kosher rock salt off the shelf
packs incision with halite crystals

my hand stings as he wraps gauze tightly
my hand burns as he shrouds gauze with adhesive
he rotates my wrist   pokes at the dressing
pulls a rubber glove over my hand
fastens an elastic around its base   thrice

Wimpy grins   orders me back to work
Nonnina pinches my cheek   rubs my shoulder
asks if I mind skinning her eel after deboning
I swab blood off her package of polpo
wipe the Wüsthof   *it will be my pleasure*

To Katrina, wherever you are, xoxoxo

I drive the Mass Pike past your city
well, it was your city in 1969
we were juniors in high school
a thirty mile romance meant
bus rides and walks from the station
your Dad and my Dad agreed
it was too far, too fast for novice operators

we'd eat dinner with your parents and sister
I was quizzed about school, the fish market
when they'd leave for a movie or the mall
you'd grab *Monopoly* or *Life*
open the box, arrange the board to mid-game
then we'd leap onto the couch, mouth-mash
your braces bruised my gums but I didn't care

when lips were too sore to collide
our eyes traced track light halos
my arms rested on your shoulders
your hands clasped my waist
our legs lurched until finding purchase
laughing as much as talking we defied
gravity, parents, homework, jobs

when we heard the garage door rail
a quick kiss brought us to bridge chairs
the table, the board—one of us threw dice
your Mom, Dad, sister came into the room
our faces bright red, our lips swollen
sister hugged us, your parents acted as if
they believed we were playing a game

forty-five years later I still grin
touch my tongue where carved gums
drove me into daydreams of you
while my teachers' mouths shaped lessons
or my knife skinned fillets with one stroke

The Gleaning
~ for Gerald Feldman

your uncle expected you to stride out of the forest

single engine Cessna
        no flight plan
a joyride, reward for wiping wings, digging tar from tires

                sketching with pencil
                eraser active on lines, shading
                a figure you draw awes me, you revise it seven times

three days passed
        I led five across Mt. Wachusett's trails
no laughter this climb, we found a denim shirt

                my Rubber Soul album
                back covered with Beatles' autographs
                my fantasy, your talent, not a dare, sleight of hand

our high school faculty
        lounged on rocks in jeans and t's
waited for their assignment

                touch football in grade school
                you are captain or whispering in the captain's ear
                I'm not the last one picked

our camp counselor brought his roommates
        ten miles they trekked each day
his wife cautioned against looking in the airplane

                I walk the neighborhood
                your house pangs disbelief
                we flew through the woods between our backyards

I won't remember how much time until the wreck was found

Objective ignorance

in chadar I learned to speak Hebrew
the trope and meter of prayer
The Mourner's Kaddish

obscenities for our biblical tongue
never uttered except
Holocaust films

the word *MAVET*:DEATH an early lesson
snaking its way through Torah
writings of martyrs

MAVET—gritty guttural gruesome
carrier of unknown fear
hidden golem

I

too young to be told ill is terminal
too young to attend funerals
too young to shovel dirt

the final mitzvah burying our own
denied to a shadow flitting
cross Nana's lawn

Riding through the Glen

put Rascal Dog down today

his four people lay palms on him
Eileen speaks in monotones
squeezes loose flesh
with thumb and index
urges needle into vein

Rascal's eyes	raindrops
body	mudslide
fiery joints	quenched

Eileen rubs our backs
tears on her cheeks

we leave him still

lying on the table

23

Toni tutors townies

note: turret boys–denizens (all genders) of dormitory tower parlors

girl darts into Toni's dorm room
strips down to panties
sits posture perfect on his stool
Toni asks s*o who are we today?*
how much thigh shall we show?
I'll prop up your titties,
design a Delilah neckline.
let's try your hair to the side:
trim the bangs, straighten that curl.

fluent tunics adorn Toni:
scoop deep-V one-shoulder keyhole
polyester satin chiffon silk
he loves loaning wardrobe to pals.
we'll go with a light base,
bare pink lipstick but smoky eyes.
heads will turn, hopefully that boy,
but remember boys have no clue!
she mouths *kiss* scampers out his door.

turret boys stare at her shimmy
until she skips up the stairs.
Toni elbows onto the couch,
reaches for a reefer passing by.
boy says *gonna have blue balls.*
Toni smiles and inhales,
slides his feet on the table.
robe too loose he sticks out a bit–
turret boys couldn't care.

that night, Toni returns to the turret,
right eye bruised lip split.
what happened? ask the boys.
Toni snorts *ran into a couple townies.*
they tried to kick the shit out of me
figured I'd grovel 'n cry not fight
uh-uh, I was raised in Bed-Stuy!
drop of blood drips down his chin—
they were afraid they were me.

Ray, six-feet two, shoulders that carried kegs like cans—
charcoal skin, knee holed jeans, red t-shirt, vest populated
by power pins.
       his girlfriend Rebecca—minister's daughter, albino white,
       a wisp wearing peasant blouses, gypsy skirts.
       in heels, her head caressed his collarbone.
first year of college, greenhorns in dormitories.

a slick nine ball shark, Ray collected quarters at the pool table.
       most of the guys were flush East Coast whites.
       he grew up in a prole Midwestern ghetto.
sinking the eight ball, Ray would grin and say
       the black one always ends up in the hole.
his ash stetson had steel studs, an Eldridge Cleaver hatband.
       when we talked about the draft and *Vi-et-nam,*
       Ray lectured about brothers immolated by the Cong.
if we countered with Jews in cattle cars or shetl boys as cannon fodder,
Ray would pop a ball, shake his chin side to side, shut his mouth.

at Muddy Waters, a bartender ignored him to serve whites.
       we grabbed the guy, told him to give Ray a beer now!
he looked up into the stolid face, hat brim cocked a tad,
drew the draught.
       Ray wouldn't brook our anger—
       said it wasn't Ours but His.
he was one of us but we were never of him.

one night in the poolroom, a bottle of Boones Farm Apple appeared.
       those that could hack sweet vinegar took swigs.
       Ray knocked back half the bottle.
       three games later, the swiggers knew the wine was spiked.
Ray never did acid, didn't even smoke the occasional joint.
he started talking about men with ropes stalking the windows.
hands shaking, he dropped his cue, ran out into the quad.

we found him on his back, thrashing in dirt, flailing arms and legs.
afraid he might run into a wall or the street or a glass door,
      six of us pinned him to the grass.
      Ray kept tossing me off his shoulder but I hung on.
an ambulance wailed in, all flashing lights and siren.
Ray bucked even harder until the paramedics needled his arm.

forty years later, we gather without Ray.
he dropped out of school, out of our lives.
      one of us says Ray is homeless in Soulard.
who spiked that bottle crashes the conversation.
it's a spirited debate, townie or prankster or stranger.
      I say nothing

Summer in St. Louis
~ August 1972

Kali, Amber, & I dance rockers as a trio.
Slow dances, Kali & I take turns with Amber.
We aren't quite equilateral, more right.
Holding Amber close, rosewater and Charlie
clash with Old Spice and perspiration.
Amber–slinky red dress, black satin belt
Kali & me–cutoff jeans, stained t's.
Amber curtsies after each number.
Kali whispers in my ear *You got no chance,*
but I do. I know she's right.

We weave out of the club at 2:00 am
hacking stale lager, cigarette fumes.
Across the street, the Switzer's factory
twists the early morning away.
St. Louis summer, air so dense
we swallow licorice with each breath.
We're smart, we're lucky
drank just enough so the rank reek
don't drag the beer out. On the street
Amber pecks Kali & me good night, leaving
us to hunt trouble in the alleys.

Blocks from the Mississippi, we taste clay
feel grains fill filaments in our nostrils.
Kali grabs my hand, how can I refuse?
She pirouettes me, gives me a sloppy
tobacco-brew-bourbon kiss, whispers a
husky *You kiss like a girl,* but it's not that.
She's more boy than me, the leader
hair on her head shorter than mine
hair under her arms longer, bushy, trailing a
randy musk–vinegar, garlic, ginger.

At The Gateway Arch, we scout for police
climb a fence, ease onto moist turf
race for the base in the gloom.
It's our civic duty, our rite of passage.
We drop shorts and briefs, tangle
to the moon lit side, pee on the Arch.
My urine smells like the boys locker room.
Kali, upwind, is splashing an earthy funk.
I breathe deeply, she laughs, pokes my side.
We shake, bounce, air won't dry us.

Kali rotates her hips side-to-side
sliding on her bottoms, mine pull right up.
She straps one arm around my hip
points the other at the Sculpture Fountain.
Time to cool off, you smell like shit!
I try *Oh yeah, you're a delicate flower.*
Naw, flower needs sun. She fled for home.
Too dark to play dirty games with her petals.
Kali slaps me, sprints, *tour jetes* into water.
I trip over the sill, flop into the fountain.

We splash, gather waves to drench the other.
Kali's braless, she's always badass braless.
Barbed nipples glower in the spotlights.
She laughs, vents water into my distracted mouth.
Spitting chlorine, my tongue wags, I groan,
sit in the water, stare at Zeus behind Kali.
I lean against Aphrodite's foot, gurgle.
We see lights flashing along the river road.
Kali yanks my hand, we sprint to shadows
cross the street, slip into Union Station.

We dog shake in the marble entrance
stamp our feet, bleed water into the carpet.
Staying on the runner to a staircase
we bound down a flight, twin squishes
each marble step, trail of Ked-prints.
The lobby, larger than two football fields
three stories tall, muffles our paces.
On a pine pew in a granite alcove
we sit, pant, Kali sticks her tongue out.
Even in shade, mocking me with her nipples.

Listening for cop shoe squeaks
an odor—fetid sweat, piss, plus a rancid
mystery element, paints our throats.
We taste the air, follow the backwash
under the pew. Kali's lighter finds a hobo
eyes frozen, lips open, dribbled blood
shirt caked with mud, vomit, brown gunk.
Flashlights illuminate the bum body. Fists
jerk us to our feet. Cops eye the corpse
grumble *Game's over kids. Now you GIT!*

pied pipers

i.

Alligator Alley, midnight, two ribbons west
reflectors, white lines, headlights puncture
                                    pitch dark
            speed limit seventy miles per hour
glance at dash, read ninety, ninety in nether
            twin vermilion rays glow in vast gloom
slow to eighty, let the car ahead trailblaze

ii.

recollect running a turnpike blackout blizzard
draft a sixteen-wheeler, gap for mud flaps' spray
            glare of tunnel's high pressure bulbs blind
            exit a velvet cleft slashed by volleys
                                    of snow
                shadow the trailer's taillights
if that trucker dives off a cliff, fates are joined

iii.

unlike boys bouncing down Madison Gulf
new moon 1am, wrist torches, sodden path
    Thad tracks two dancing gleams
                                    warned of
                fallen limbs, loose rocks
Joe's beam on the right wavers, vanishes
Richard's glint to the left arcs, disappears
                Thad scans murk from ledge brow
The trail don't go that way. No shortcuts
                                    after dark!

Bullseye

Joe likes his martini dry, *Just dip the olive in vermouth, willya?*
married ladies seeking the forbidden—initials on his calendar.
it's summer, he's at South Schroon—the lake house
        with listing stairs, windows propped open
        by Beefeater bottles, slivers anywhere you lean.
the barn hides paint, palettes, easels, shrouded canvasses.

after lunch, we drink Narragansett tall boys—
my gift, gaunt beer from the hometown.
        when we have ten empties, it's time to bowl.
        we don't have a ball but a cantaloupe is handy.
        to our eyes, it rolls straight and true.
        after a dozen frames, Joe nods at the china cabinet—
open the top left drawer, bring me my knife.
I hand him a foot long bowie knife, oiled and edged.
he tosses the cantaloupe in the air.
a flick of the wrist, it splits in two.
        My father sent me this knife when I was overseas.
        Told me to use it to kill Nazis. How the fuck was I
        going to kill Nazis with a knife at 28,000 feet?
        Throw it at a Messerschmidt? Bean an ack ack gunner?

Joe fluffs my hair, *you're a real hippie, huh?*
Dylan and Baez? Those two are punks. Never paid dues.
Hippies are copycats. You're all ersatz beats.
        I visit his Greenwich Village loft.
        there is a fragrance, sugary but musty
        on his clothes, in the air, on Coke bottle butts.
        he hands me Ginsberg, Levertov, Ferlinghetti, Bukowski.
        This is real poetry not that crap they teach in school.
        any book in his digs is mine.
        I choose Upton Sinclair, the man in the signed photograph.
the next July Fourth at Schroon, after a swim,
he rails on flower children.
my response—beats are just watered down '20s Socialists.
he smiles, nods, clasps my shoulder.

32

after breakfast, before beer-martinis-weed,
he pulls out a pair of hand carved bows.
I grab a couple of quivers, Joe a fresh cigar.
   in front of the beach sit two targets.
   my spot is less than a stone's throw from the bullseye.
   his, across the street past the edge of the property.
on a good day, I put two arrows in the outer rings.
he always buries five in the center circle.

   that moment is the only moment I see the bombardier:
peering through the Norden sight, chomping a cigar,
   flak exploding, fighters raking his airplane.
wails from trapped buddies in a crippled B-24.
   gunners return fire, a scream—one of his crew hit.
rocked side-to-side, tossed up and down,
   he lines up the target, exhales, pulls the release,
reports—*bombs away.*

Casualty and Medic reconnect on Facebook
~ for Francis Xavier Weyerich

I wanted to crawl out of that valley–didn't want to get
on the chopper–cross-fire from three ridges.

It was like a comic book–zing, pop, zip-zip-zip.

While the Huey lifted, I waited for Charley to waste us.

You lay on a stretcher, flight medic checking the dressing–I
hoped you weren't gonna lose that leg–blood congealed
in the rice paddy–it was hard to find your wound.

You sat on the middle bench–medic stitched your temple.

We landed at the hospital, you triaged one way,
me another–never saw you again.

There was blood covering your head–I didn't know how bad
you were hit, if the round fucked up your brain.

Don't remember much–I was Mr. Two Eyes blinking at
the sun, my helmet flipped off and the eye was dead.

I saw the round ricochet off the rim, shatter into your face–
don't know how you put that compress on your eye–
don't remember your hands leaving my leg.

Couldn't find my helmet when we headed to the LZ–
spent months embroidering that liner–
always wondered what killed my eye.

For forty years, I wondered if you were alive–if you could
see–if you knew your own name.

For forty years, I feared you lost your leg or life—
I feared I failed you.

How could you have failed me? Blood was flowing out
of the socket, there was shrapnel in your forehead.

It was my job.

Johnny, Billy, and I build forts out of wooden blocks.
        conceal green army men in notches, under circle cut outs.
        play artillery with jax balls.
            last general with a man standing wins.

we save our quarters for the Army-Navy store.
        buy Ka-Bars, half shelter tents, fart sacks.
        they were good enough for Ike's boys.

every week, we watch *Combat* on black and white TV.
        our favorite episode features an All-Star pitcher.
            his platoon is ambushed, he dives into a foxhole
                cradling his shoulder. Soldiers die.
            Sarge challenges him to a fistfight, bloodies his nose.
        they shake hands, patrol into a firefight.
the pitcher whips grenade after grenade into Nazi bunkers,
        routs the Krauts, ruins his arm, rescues buddies.

Cousin Marvin hides a Jap gas mask in his attic,
        a shattered Arisaka rifle.
            I ask him if he killed a Nip.
                Marvin bores a hole between my eyes.
            stammering, he taunts with words I don't get.
stomps off. won't look at me for a month.

the night before Dad ships out to the Pacific,
        Uncle Danny takes him to see *Objective, Burma!*
            Errol Flynn loses most of his troopers,
        severed cocks stuffed in mouths before death.
Dad tells Danny he'll make it home.

1969. I march to a hearing, summoned by the headmaster.
sideburns too long, hair below the collar,
book bag stuffed with anti-war leaflets.
we plan a county wide school strike.
I climb marble stairs,
stomach taut, sweat sticks shirt to torso,
turn the corner to the head's office.
hear Dad's voice drill through the door
so why are you afraid of protest?

Anaphora for Ann

I love that we want to share rooms that look like we live in them.

I love that you enjoy laundry and hate grocery shopping.

I love that you punched the dandy in DeGaulle who elbowed his way through the line pulling my bag and the shoulder attached out of joint and when he turned red faced for a confrontation your scowl scared him away.

I love how you sped outside to help the young woman who was escaping her boyfriend's car.

I love your laugh when you're looking at pictures of babies or puppies.

I love how you join me in discussions of fictional characters as if they were intimate friends.

I love that on our honeymoon in Woodstock, we drank three carafes of Chablis then staggered around town invading gallery after gallery until we found a statue of a fox in repose.

I love how you giggle when a book amuses you but can't explain why.

I love how your shirt tags stick up and I get to surreptitiously tuck them in place.

I love how you trim my eyebrows when wiry hairs braid briar patches.

I love that you are calm, analytic, and in control when I go to see the oncologist even when you're worried but don't want me to know until after the appointment.

I love how you sparkle when you gaze at our sons and how strong you are when one of them is sick, has been wronged, or is wandering off track.

I love that you rushed to nurse Nana Sarah when she had a heart attack and arrived days before her children.

I love that you could answer every one of Rabbi Goldstein's questions in conversion class which he loved because his student cared.

I love your vocation, how you helped people dealing with abuse, PTSD, depression, and violence heal their lives.

I love your mischievous smile that indicates a loverly surprise is on its way.

I love that WE trumps I.

I love our 37 years together and imagining those to come.

I love you. You are my life. I am your me.

Apple of my eye

mating season in the Everglades
apple snails scale reeds
paste egg sacks six inches above
currents   fish jowls   snake fangs

1992   snails keep climbing
to forty inches where reeds rock in breezes
secure their sacks before rappelling
(do they kiss them goodbye?)

malacologists hunt swamps for clues
until Hurricane Andrew levels levees
defiles drainage   displaces woodlands   departs
water level thirty-four inches higher

a son is born   needs blood to survive
head bruised   warped by forceps
we field phone calls   shovel snow
the dog carves trails around drifts

school labels son lazy   he won't stay seated
a prescribed pill vaults him to top of class
in test scores   defending the pitch
slipping out windows   finding easy friends

we wait for a garage door to open at 3am
smell clothing   hair   in the guise of a hug
listen for slurs from swaggering tongue
(should we kiss him goodnight?)

"There comes a time when suddenly you realize
that laughter is something you remember
and that you were the one laughing."
~ Marlene Dietrich

"A wild patience has
taken me this far."
~ Adrienne Rich

The trial survey
~ a study to perceive whether needles palliate pain from radiation

Every fourth garnish, a research questionnaire precedes acupuncture.

Q. How often do you evacuate?
A. Too often.

Q. Do you have trouble sleeping?
A. No, trouble waking.

Q. Can you identify oranges by scent?
A. Everything smells like metal or sweat.

Q. Can you drink an 8 ounce glass of water in 15 minutes?
A. Only if I pour it in my PEG tube.

Q. How would you rate your pain on a scale of 1 to 5?
A. Consistent.

Q. Do you feel ill?

> Lost 20 pounds.
> Mouth and throat are The Sahara Desert—
> all but one saliva gland burnt out.
> Tongue and inner cheeks cracked, cut, lesions, sores.
> A sip is more fiendish than a chin-up with dumbbells
> tacked to belt.
> Feeding myself I visit Never Never Land and
> wake with face in puddle on tray.
> Spit out foul fluid, vomit into sink.
> Shower or no shower, smell like garbage left too long
> in the sun and wonder how anyone can sit
> near me even though everyone
> tells me my aroma is a-ok.
> Pillowcase is decorated with sundry tints drooled,
> tongued, belched into perverse patterns.
> Magic Mouthwash numbs my mouth,
> fifteen minutes of bliss.

43

I am in a microcellular war.
Body littered with collateral damage,
        friendly fire my battle buddy.
Outlook is fierce, weak, determined, trampled.
Hurts to laugh but—scorched neck like bad makeup
        in horror films—does my gait describe
        drunkenness or doddering?—
        hiccups make dogs bark.
Feel sad for your frowns, but I fight, wrack and wreck my guts.
Will kill squeamish cell carcinoma, that alien training traitors
        within my flesh.
I am a survivor. My fellow warriors fall while I trudge on.
        We chortled at our foes, wrapped each others' pain
        into eloquent forget-me-nots, told each other to
        Stay Strong.
Am I guilty? wonder why I'm still here?

A. No. I don't feel ill.

My infusion nurse smiles as she releases the clamp on my pic line and invites Cisplatin in

veins chill at the port–I shuck off a shiver
earns me a hot blanket–cup of tea
tongue tingles–a creeping plows the skull
just below–where the bald spot roamed
drink my cup–creeping seeps deeper
a pulsing tick adheres–to the brain

shut my eyes breathe–stale air
the IV pump whirs–thrilling scale
a familiar tune–a familiar room
my nurse brings–bottles of water
five minutes since–I peed
swallow flat–metallic fluid

tick embraces–entire cortex
stem emits cotton–yes cotton
drip by drip engulfs–each lobe
the nerves limp–bump in line
try to read a–paragraph
sentences–dug ditches

sunshine pours–in southern panes
ice forms on–roofs' snow
melts and freezes–melts and freezes
I am cottonball brain–it feels it feels
lights have halos–fan tickles my skin
my stomach trills–I fart

nurse buttons–my wool shirt
I have three–blankets tucked about me
Boston Red Sox–cap freezer boots
rabbit-lined gloves wait–on the table
wind whacks the building–rails windows
I clasp my elbows prepped–for Winter

the janitor, swaddled in gown gloves mask, cleans my room.
we trade *Adiós. Mañana.* as he closes my door,
the door covered with placards: GOWN GLOVES MASKS
REQUIRED–DOOR SHUT AT ALL TIMES!

the nurse takes my vitals.
her breathing is loud under fabric.
her fingers through latex pinch my skin.
she warns me *the hospitalist is coming to see you.*

the hospitalist swirls into the room.
coughs into her elbow, says *excuse me!*
I gaze at her and six medical students,
no masks no gloves no gowns–door wide open.

the hospitalist reads my chart to her charges,
pauses to ask me if I'm in pain.
my answer is a query about masks gloves gowns.
waving a naked palm, she replies *I'm the doctor!*

my white blood cell count is negative.
three bags of antibiotics link to my IV line.
my temperature remains 102°.
swallowing a sip of water is torture.

the hospitalist prods my belly.
applies a stethoscope to my chest.
asks me to breathe deeply, *and once more.*
she coughs turning to instruct the students.

the hospitalist decides to check my port-o-cath,
peels off three layers of protective sealing,
pokes with ungloved fingers,
lightly taps the dressing back in place, unsealed.

the hospitalist prescribes a series of medications.
one I am allergic to grants days of diarrhea.
she coughs, pirouettes on her heel,
leads her entourage out the door–left open.

the nurse returns with pills and water,
sees my port dressing open to the air,
tears it off growling anatomical expletives–
bathes the incision region with antiseptic,

layers new bandages, seals them to skin.
scrawls on the chart for several minutes.
tucks in my blanket, adjusts pillows, muttering
can't believe that bitch did this to MY patient!

Tefillah sheni
~ for Marsha Kunin

I.

curl air up nostrils, infuse lungs
cradle breath, stretch cage
      release
search the unseen
pace, silent metronome
seek what can solely be
tremble at nearness of unknown
divine ridden on moments of piety
      faith posts the unnamed
      no reins, no bridle, bareback

II.

      infusion room corner
I lounge with hollow-cheeked man

we exchange pleasantries:
location, stage of tumors
      treatment protocol
      prolificacy of bowels
port, PEG appliances

he grins out the window
girl 'n boy balance on fence posts
      giggle as they tumble
he embraces my hand with his(cold)
winks at our nurse

before I'm uncoupled from IVs
he tells me he is terminal

chemo can contain his tumors
          for now
in the next year and a half
maybe a new drug

                    the sun kisses his chin
                              marveling, he affirms
God Bless You

On the nature of bliss

these pine trees, old friends
some, chest high our first visit
have lower branches beyond our reach.

I follow these paths on moonless nights,
soles of my feet sense gravel-dirt-tar,
navigate curves by shadows,
starlight reflects from the lake.

this cottage, ours–one August week a year.
same kitchen stove as the house I was raised.
bookshelf with volumes of logarithm tables.
map of Sebago, crease along Raymond Neck.

this year, naps on the couch harbored by my dog.
rocking on a long tabled porch facing the beach trail.
I pour formula into my feeding tube,
watch running children chased by parents.
dogs bark, babies cry, teens screech
going to the lake for sun, sand, swim.
I must stay dry, must stay in shade.

two months of "recovery"–
teaspoons of baby apple sauce, yogurt,
scrambled eggs, vanilla pudding–
my swallows, fingernails on sunburned skin.

two months of
ten minute shuffles–
past two houses and the synagogue

two months of reading a six-line verse of poetry—
twice
three times
four
of reading just the first line—
twice
three times
four
of tossing book at the floor.

here, with my family,
even my shoebox of pills reclines.
my son eats a Maine boiled dinner—
sweet corn, red potatoes, steamers, lobster.
I share the wisdom of my youth—
how to crack and extract the pink meat.

next week, a visit with the oncologist,
blood work, x-rays, vitals, hose up nose.
food tastes like overripe copper.
water—stored in a rusty thermos.

today, a breeze from the lake carries
pine cones, suntan lotion, hamburger sizzle,
splashing, giggles, a boat on the far shore.
eyes closed, world still, I am

         paddle to the ladder on the downwind side
             four rungs but use only one to ascend
                the wooden float with a decoy owl

               azure sky to the east, no haze on the saddle
          between Mount Washington and Mount Jefferson
      sunburst and breeze dry body and swimsuit
    stretch fingertips to touch clouds
accordion down onto oak planks

hands cup wind, toes flicker the range
      Mother Sebago rocks the float
           pine trees on the beach
               block and reveal, block and reveal
                sun rays, eyes close

                  waves lap the float, whisper on the sand

              a motorboat parts the lake, drowns birdcalls
            the float seesaws, seesaws and settles
        boat fades, currents return to cradle
      sun retreats, surface fuses orange glaze
water sighs, planks creak, barrels moan

                a loon calls

double vision

      crawl the hall
left eye patched
      shift left
shoulder slams door frame
      shut both eyes

      parse line one
line two cracks syntax
      parse line one
focus on first letter
      push eyes down
lost in paragraph

      football on TV
twin quarterbacks bark
      ticker climbs screen
blink   wink   bat
      tube is Pollock paint

      key email
right eye patched
      the the dup'ed
deep of the pool
      minus an end
this is prolbem

      will I write post stroke?
I can't rein in
      thinking in rhyme
is that a crime?
      merely sublime?

my high school buddies ask me what I was thinking
as they pick me up off the bathroom floor when I
miss the toilet seat while trying to sit down

St. Louis ice storm
BJ & I grasp the gauntlet
grab six packs of Grolsch
slog our way to the I-44 overpass
for each vehicle that glides off the egress
we will gurgle a beer

Missouri drivers shrug at deluge
shake snow gust's glove
but black ice's guile
they never recognize
car toggles tarmac to field
before we pop a top   again   again

we try with gusto to remain
unswerving to our pilgrimage
six beers in thirty minutes an ungodly task
even for two well-greased collegians
we give as cars 7 and 8 skip grade
begin staggering to our digs

glacial slides   glaring sidewalks   should not
plague boys weaned in northern winter
I totter into a garage door
BJ stumbles over a gate
winged cans gambol in the road
we grimace at gluteal gashes

On the nature of learning how to swallow after thirty-five radiation treatments to the throat
~ from Emily Dickinson's "To make a prairie"

Three sips of water each hour says Doctor—
squats for the throat muscles,
clean jerks for the tongue,
rehabilitation for ravaged tissue.

Timer buzzes, reset for sixty minutes.
Palm grips the Poland Spring bottle.
So thirsty, a long swig Adam's apple bobbing—
God, to be able to do that again!

First sip, cross a prairie,
flat, hidden holes, shifting sand.
Snag on a rusty chain link fence,
wire rips as I move.

Second sip, crawl a muddy path
along a waterfall. Climb two steps,
slide down one, breeze splatters drops.
They burn as they evaporate.

Third sip, traverse a switchback.
Goldenrod bushes tent the trail.
Brush a branch, anger a bee.
Its stinger tunnels deep, lingers.

Thanks for the draft but alcohol is verboten.

Lend me your Guinness.
Let me sniff its bouquet.
      Yeah, I'd love a pint.
No beer is bad enough, but no mouthwash,
      no Nyquil?
Alcohol is the ticket to recur oral cancer.
The irony? Before diagnosis,
      I woke at 5:00 am.
      Exercised for an hour.
      Didn't drink. Didn't smoke.
      Ate a vegan diet.
I'm not drawing lots when it comes to tumors.
You drink a stout for me.
I'll inhale this Americano.
Given a choice between coffee or booze—
      coffee has always won.

I grew up thinking poison was bad.
As a teen, wine offered a challenge.
Then 'Gansetts, ouzo, tequila, Glenlivet.
Mornings reminded me—
      pounding temples,
      gurgling stomach—
      sometimes a floor to clean.
Got older. The beat of cleats on pavement.
Price of that ticket, no spirits in the blood.

Chemotherapy is loving poison.
Liters of chemicals in bags marked—
   Wear gloves. Do not let liquid
   come in contact with skin—
  pump through veins.
Lights flicker, IV machine warbles,
   forehead stretches wide,
    eyes pop left-right-right-left.
Wife asks me a question. I begin to answer.
Volunteer pushes a food cart.
    Vanilla pudding—lovely!
Wife taps my shoulder. *Huh?*

Radiation weakens teeth.
Twice a day, I fill latex trays—
   molds of my dentition—
   with concentrated fluoride.
They lounge in my mouth for a half hour.
Spit-spit-spit says my dentist. *Don't swallow!*
   Fluoride. Poison. But don't rinse!
I have one saliva gland left.
Dry hack into the sink.

Before diagnosis,
   a morning mug of espresso.
Following treatment,
   a demitasse spoon.
After three months, a single shot.

JAMA publishes a study:
   Coffee's poison
   inhibits oral cancer—
   ah, Hobson's choice.

Gimme a quad espresso over ice, please.
   Black. No sugar.

"You only live twice:
Once when you are born
And once when you look death in the face"
~ *You Only Live Twice*, Ian Fleming

every morning:
a shake of the shoulder   or   the buzzing of an alarm clock on a
dresser across the room, I must get out of a warm bed to hit the kill
button   or   the cry of a baby / lover   or   a friend vomiting after
imbuing Ouzo   or   a fall off the ledge of a skyscraper, I flip, sidewalk
coming closer until I inhale a shriek, jerk my skull, realize it all was a
dream

                                    face another day

times I almost die:
          driving on a highway from Jefferson City to St. Louis after
drinks and appetizers with a secretary celebrating her last day   Jason
Dog on the seat beside me sleeping   my eyes heavy   the car lurches
a view of a ditch on the side of I-70   I pull the car bouncing 70 miles
per hour into the hammer lane   heart pounds for four exits until I
decide to calm down with coffee

          twenty-five feet up climbing a rock wall at East Park on the 4th
of July   kids start throwing firecrackers cherry bombs M80s at me   I
sprawl for cover under protruding boulders fingers toes slip but I find
holds at last breath   finally reach the top of the wall   watch the kids
run away squealing

          surgeon says odds are 70 percent that cancer will painfully
drain my life   wife & I should treasure our remaining time   surgeon
has no clue what caused the cancer   wants to slit my throat   carve out
the tumor   *oh, you will not be able to raise your arms above the shoulder again*
but that's a small price to pay for days   surgeon advises that an oncologist
will want to pump chemo propel radiation   that will make a more
difficult, less effective extraction of the growth so surgeon will fit me
in next week   procedure is only $10,000   *sorry, I don't accept insurance*

Ace of spades: cancer

Neck lymph nodes spawn walnuts. Surprising the speed they swell. No
doubt about prognosis. The rhythm of treatment is not unknown—
infusion room reservations, benign mummy throat wraps. Chemo
transforms paragraphs into Möbius crossword puzzles. Radiation
elevates curling to the pinnacle of heart pounding entertainment.
Balancing the checkbook not attempted.

Queen of clubs: stroke

                The startle,
                      fanfare for a burst brain vessel.
Moments of veiled confusion,   litter from nightmarish creases.
                Double vision, a lash-latched
        onto eyeball.
                Turning down wrong roads, absent
        lapses.
                Losing words, having a
                    bad day.
                Writing verse, drooping
      participles.
                Missed appointment, their clerical
        miscue.
                Flawed recognition, abscesses in others'
cerebration.

Jack of hearts: 10th plague

Heeding that murmur only my child utters
    —not in regret   but   while he falls
over the wall   from a ten-story terrace—
    rouses faith's single-edge razor
        to flail my skin.
Following him, the   only viable course.

Savant suave

I seldom spill on my shirt, when I do you stare.
Grunts emit from my mouth, some resemble speech.
My face is your face, if I wink you glance away.

Da orders coffee bagels, we listen for our name.
The barista calls, I pick the tray up, yowl a thanks.
She serves me often, smiles *You're Welcome Tim.*

Think I don't hear you, whispering to your beau?
He giggles at my gait, mimics the angle of my chin.
I watch him with other girls, whispering in their ears.

You both read with a dictionary, I rarely need one.
Can he write poems to your dimples, does he desire?
Kindness isn't silence, talk with me like you talk to him.

Permit me to sit at your table, drink a latte.
Those calculus problems, slide them to my side.
Before you curse one, I can decipher them all.

When I'm close, your eyes seek the floor.
You tell cronies be nice, caution my body is a trap.
I'm the one who's free, ever certain where I stand.

the crone evaluates her
Occupational Therapist

pink boots
purple laces

puce polo shirt
crest over the heart

taupe trousers
tad too thick in the waist

touch of blue eyeshadow
rose lipstick on teeth

brittle blonde mane
boy's page cut

no ring on finger
should have three kids by now

Driving Test

Ma'am, I'm going to say a name and street address.
You repeat it after me and I'll ask you to recall it later.
Ma'am repeats the first name, twice.

> *at sixteen, her father teaches her how to drive*
> *she is a bonnet taller than four feet*
> *he puts his right hand on the steering wheel*
> *lays his left elbow on the open windowsill*
> *insists she mimic, left arm wrenched up forty-five degrees*

Ma'am, two shapes will flash on the screen.
You must look then identify.

> *sixty-one years ago, her first car*
> *a rusting Rambler American*
> *three-speed on the column*
> *son and daughter jump in the rear*
> *baby boy lies in basinet on front floor*
> *she drives the car only in second gear*
> *back seat kids bumped off the bench*

Ma'am, here's a stoplight. As the color goes green-yellow-red,
I want you to pump this brake pedal appropriately.
Ten times the lights shine, ten times she slaps the pedal.
Ma'am, you average .96 of a second. Registry cutoff is .54.

> *how could anyone hit it faster?*

Ma'am watches the examiner shift left-right-left on a stool.

> *she shuts her eyes, glides her convertible*
> *along Florida parkways flanked by banyan trees*
> *she cruises the hammer lane, passes slow pokes*
> *breeze whisks through her silk kerchief*

Ma'am raises her chin, peers in the examiner's eyes.
> *I can find my own way out.*

Exit 16

paralleled by train tracks, crumbled factories
tarmac alleys paved with shattered glass

the shunned 'hood–tenants evicted, cars towed
power cut off at laundromat, food co-op

its tenements–mansions with aristocratic bones
stripped, reborn, lawns purged of knotweed

potholes vanish, streetlights vacate shadows.
swings, slides supplant a salvage lot

Central Avenue, rechristened MLK Jr Blvd–
church whitewashed, spire spit-polished

Cpl Jim on his furlough Thanksgiving 1942 - BROWN PHOTO SERVICE | Minneapolis, Minn. | DEC 11 1942
~ From a photograph found in an antique store

Sonny-Jim, electric wheelchair in rabbit mode, launches over the curb, jams into Kelley Square, the conflux of six roads, a vehicular no-man's land. Cars lock their brakes, truck air horn pulses, Sonny-Jim runs straight and true to THE SPOT—dead center, hub of the wheel, no cover.

A police officer holds her palm out to stop traffic, her partner stirs vehicles around the hazard. The officer kneels down, eye-to-eye with Sonny-Jim, notes the M-1943 Field Jacket, Sergeant stripes, Silver Star Service Ribbon.

Sir, do you know where you are?

Damn straight I do! I'm on THE SPOT. Before we shipped out, the Sonny Boys-Herman, Saul, Jim met here. We shimmied in a circle, hand slapping over hand—Hi-de-ho Sonny, what's buzzin', cousin?—Get a load of Sonny, he's one decked out hepcat!—Sonny, you are the ace ducky shincracker!

Sonny-Herman was a Marine PFC. Bayoneted Japs at the Battle of Alligator Creek until a bullet cut him down. Lt. Sonny-Saul assaulted Gold Beach, fought his way across France and Germany, wounded three times. They made him a Captain in Nuremberg but during the celebration spin in his Jeep, a neck high trip wire decapitated him. Me—Corporal Sonny-Jim, I landed on Juno Beach. Had a nifty march across France carting my greaser—until the Battle of Nancy. A Rhino 88 blew off my right arm and leg. Shrapnel's still in my side. I raked a bunker pretty good before they popped me.

Sir, we need to move you into safety. Do you have family I can call?
A friend?

My family's all dead. I'm the youngest. Never married. Who'd want me? You gotta wake me up from across the room. Shake my sleeping shoulder and I'll slug you. Guess you could call the VFW Post. No friends there. They're all dead, too. All that's left are some Vietnam boys and kids from The Gulf Wars. Can't understand any of 'em. But they always buy me beer and shots. Before you move me, I have a final mission on THE SPOT. This photo, it earned being snuffed out where we shook.

Sonny-Jim pulls a creased black and white photo from his pocket, kisses it, drops it on pavement, runs his chair over and back, over and back. *See, just like us.*

The last Zero ace testifies

~ for samurai of the sky, Kaname Harada, veteran of Pearl Harbor, Midway, and Guadalcanal

nothing is as terrifying as war
I conjure the faces of men I killed
fathers, sons, I never knew or abhorred

until I die, I warn against my tour
dream of American bombers I spilled
nothing is as terrifying as war

divine visions, no defense to ignore
our children by honored horrors drilled
fathers, sons, I never knew or abhorred

war turned me into slaughterer of corps
not Bushido I hungered to fulfill
nothing is as terrifying as war

statesmen born after The Pacific War
must avoid crusades deemed Emperor's will
fathers, sons, I never knew or abhorred

faded memories, disowned-spurned-deplored
glamorous dreams like prewar leaders milled
nothing is as terrifying as war
fathers, sons, I never learned to abhor

The original sin

Your voice called. I said *Hineni (Here I am)*.
You commanded. I clutched my knife.

There I was with the blade at Isaac's throat.
A bed of tinder for his cradle or pyre.
He did not squirm, smiled into my face, trusted me.

Your emissary hooked my wrist just before I sliced his throat.
How in Your name could I even think to do Your bidding?
Who was I? Who would I be?

You cause a ram to appear. Albino. Yellow eyes. Alive,
        eagerly flaunting his jugular.
I spill his blood, red on olive branches.

For You.

Your covenant: my descendants will be
        as numerous as grains of sand.
The desert?
What world do I germinate?
Will my seed seek to live as angels

or have Your eyes?

You proclaim *there is no afterlife,*
        no heaven, no hell, just a name lives on.

Perhaps it's found if I slit all our throats.

Rosh Hashanah 5775 – Yom Reeshone

Adam wouldn't have eaten that apple
it was the way Eve dressed   or
how she flipped her head shaking *NO*
fending off Adam egged on by his
wingman the snake

Sarah wept in her tent
waiting on Abraham and Isaac
her intuition trawled
fists holding rags   she was the one
who bled that day

in the sanctuary someone beseeches
"too many women on the bimah"
another she chants Torah   he
casts groans like crumbs   davens
Avinu Malkeinu

***

Yom Reeshone first day
bimah a raised platform where the Torah is read (altar)
casts groans like crumbs Rosh Hashanah tradition to throw bread (sins)
   on moving water
davens chants prayers rhythmically
Avinu Malkeinu Rosh Hashanah prayer *Our Father, Our King*

"It is not with impunity that one is soft,
polished, reasonable, patient,
day after day, year after year."
~ Samuel Beckett

"There's nothing that makes you so aware of the
improvisation of human existence as a song
unfinished. Or an old address book."
~ Carson McCullers

fil de téléphone
–for Melvin Fox (1923-2014)

I hear Dad's voice the last time
walking *Crypte Archeologique de Notre-Dame*
   remnants of the Roman Empire buried
   in rubble under the cathedral.

walls, scorned by centuries, broken but vain,
intricate archways over stone paths–evidence
   of vitality, ambition, vernal faith
   in the immortality of majesty.

Dad hails me with an emphatic *HELLO!*
asking about Paris, his words stray and sag
   but he says *I love you, I'm proud of you*
   solid and enduring as granite.

My sister believes Dad's brothers are calling him to rejoin
the card game.

Today I can not rouse
     Dad
     curled under bone afghan
     profile half moon to pillow
     torso fetal skeleton
     frail his aide Lisa says
     decimated I think
     he was thin when he returned from the Pacific
          sixty-eight years ago   but in his wedding film
          he prances   bounds table to table   cover him
          with a poncho   there would've been burly ripples

Yesterday
     Dad
     sits in his recliner
     wants to walk but would topple
     Lisa says *why don't you march?*
     she backs the wheelchair over
     he holds the handles
     we lift under his shoulders   raise him   he wavers   balances
     Lisa urges *raise one foot then the other*
          c'mon, like you did in the service
     he lifts a foot half an inch   down   the other   repeats
     Lisa whispers *using both legs equally*

     Dad
     smiles
     asks about fish
     what fish? I question
     garble-fish-garble they have a beautiful menu garble-bring
          a checkbook-garble ha-garble he nods to me
     halibut? I wonder
     haddock – halibut's good too!
     he thinks he's filling orders at the fish market

Dad

pauses
looks over at his empty bed
did you do that? it's won-der-ful!
I smile and say *yes*
he begins talking to his long-gone brothers
motions to the bed again   points at a phantom
I ease a protein shake to his lips
he shakes his head *for you*
I try water drink from my glass first   he sips from his
leans back grins
don't forget fish   bring the checkbook   you need a
checkbook to pay-garble way back pick-garble-up

Dad

watches *Family Feud*
rubs hands together for FAST MONEY
echoes *aaaaaahhhhhhhnnnnttt!* at zero dollar answers
our patter rhythm matches each day before
          he doesn't yell answers
          he doesn't grimace at grotesque guesses
          he beckons to the TV barks *garble-garble*

Today

Dad still sleeps after I bring Mom home from the clinic
we nosh apple cake   cup of tea
before departing I return to him
gently shake his shoulder   a baton draped in chalk
he doesn't stir
I lean over him
subtle rancid scent   stronger than yesterday
I kiss his cheek say *I love you!*
he replies a soft *gar-uhh-ble*   same meter as me

Piss ant

high school
boys drink cans of piss-poor beer
        run to the toilet to drain their mains
                can't wait for a turn
                        swords are crossed
      twin streams geyser the bowl
shaky commingling sprays seat stall floor

                      college
            boys quaff drafts at a blues dive
                one bumps into another or
                    laughs or
                        burps
        the other   long pissed
        now adds pissed off
        pours his mug over the one's head
            who pops the other in the nose
                who grapples the pair to the
        sticky parquet   boys whistle
                applaud blood
        slur slurs
        the gladiators grope
            until breaths expressed
                rallied to their feet
                    mugs refilled
              they laud the blows
          toast their new chum
    forget why they fought

hospice vigil

geezers piss in Tranquility
disposable adult underwear

they sip water   Boost   maybe apple juice

munch graham crackers
slathered with peanut butter
hide fingers from diabetes lancets
clamp lips to foil offered pills
roll away from pulling poking prying
blend anger+recollection into chaos
the once boys surface wondering how-when
geezers count spurts of urine
no fluid demonstrations
just fresh diapers

Unreasonable

Dying doesn't live up to its press

body little more than lesion-coated skeleton
el moribundo in diapers, bowels out of control
      no food tempts
      no drink appeals
      medicine an overwrought task
he peers at family, smiles
then sleeps, snoring an eccentric whistle
vigil reconvenes
      he awakens
      nudges his walker
            to the bathroom
            or the kitchen
            or the porch
until, again incontinent, he is in bed
seeing dead relatives and conversing
      shivers but complains that it's too warm
      sweats but implores he's freezing
      sings jingles from his childhood
the holy one asks to visit but there's never a time he's awake before—
unresponsive, not the first time or the tenth time, not the first vigil or
the last he dies alone—did he know which word would be his final?
    did he know the moment both feet entered the next world?
    did he know we all came to say goodbye to his corpse?
    did he feel those warm kisses on his cold flesh?
    did he sense our hands covering his hands?
    did he hear the words we uttered?

It makes for bad TV.

BURN
~ in memory of Michael Hill

"Since we're all going to die, it's obvious that when and how don't
matter."
~Albert Camus, *L'Étranger*

*my ant begins her trek from the top of molding in a corner of the ceiling towards the
spackle near the lone light. no hesitation in her march, trail well-blazed, third trek
since i woke, only my eyes have moved. wonder if spackle is made with sugar or
whether a food fight splatted sauce up there. hard to tell in the soot. where is the
ladybug?*

sleeping bag over two blankets, still shiver
floor may be hard, but sheets burn

could gulp oxycodone, ply a morphine patch
bury the pain, might miss the punch line

thankful for my iPod, Beatles 24/7
John & George get me, peace in the space between

no more rolling to my feet to pee, sip water
pretend to pick a snack, used to crave MoonPies

have a few urinals to fill, someone can empty them someday
liquid evidence I was here, kinder than a puddle

day night noon, same light from the shade
that single bulb above, we race to see who goes out first

my money's on me, it's a long-life bulb
bet if I held it today, my fingers wouldn't burn

If they can

You, as editor, ask me for a poem for *Wind In The Willows,*
the monthly magazine of your retirement community.
I, your son-in-law, seek to have poems in print,
but turning the pages of my notebook, reject each for:
  curse-quake as beer pours over head
  hand rolled herb passes fingers to fingers
  two boys kiss at a bus stop
  a man a woman a bed loud moans
and—
  needles pierce flesh to pump poison at carcinoma
  radiation burns out saliva glands
  Super Bowl score forgotten every commercial
  death death death of infusion room fellows cousins friends

I recall a Shabbat when I read Jewish poets as a sermon.
Just before the service, a Kaddish is added to the rituals—
fresh death of a father. Family and friends fill the sanctuary.
Flipping through my chosen verses, all I find is death—
Jews and death, inseparable coupling, irresistible twinning.
One poem speaks of a bubbie looking out her bedroom window
  to a garden where her granddaughter picks lilies.
  The girl skips bed to bed, spreads out like an angel in the grass.
  When the child raises her fists to the sky, the bubbie sees
  barbed wire, numbers tattooed on wrists, her sister
  twin of the girl punching clouds, marching to the gas chamber.
Of all the poems I tab, this is the sweetest

I recall a coffeehouse when I book a young buck to open for a legend.
After his set, the boy sits next to me as the woman skips song to song.
The house sings along identifying each tune by its first notes.
He holds his head in his palms, cries *Oh shit! Just look at the crowd.*
  They're old. Can't believe I did my dirty ditties.
I rub his back, tell him *No worries, the house laughed.*
Older means they know much more about sex than you.

I never chose a poem for *Wind In The Willows*.
Hope that wasn't a disappointment.
You read my book. The themes speak for themselves.
At your shiva, the hospice aide confides in me:
you'd think most people would want to die in their sleep,
but they'd prefer to die during sex. It's an "if they can".

The other side

i.

working behind the market counter
    I cleaned fish as each customer instructed
scraped excess skin, innards into a crate
    by request, took trips to the cooler
selected a fillet as fresh as the case
    presented each side under pink lights
they nodded, smiled at this privilege
    weight approved, I slapped fish into tray
wrapped with newsprint, strip of tape to seal
price in black marker, my numbers on a packet

ii.

I stand in the mourner's waiting line
    people crowd around my family
say *excuse me* as they jostle for position
    each with words fragile as sea foam
I render replies to relieve each lamenter
    file retorts my fancy frames
wrap proffered palms with two hands
    hug to seal the transaction
before chapel, they sign names in black ink
address and phone, no errors in accounting

Shamayim

Hell, a mirrored honky-tonk,
splintered in actions not taken.
       All the free beer you must drink
       to dowse salt impaled
       in pretzels, barbecued crisps.
Pay toilets accept correct change.
Seven shiny pennies in your clutch
don't quarter.

Heaven, a quilted hammock,
stranded in mercies not plotted.
       A buffet, fragrant marrow
       to quench pangs fertile in
       regret, forlorn weakness.
Grilled egg yolks signal intentions.
Green apples served with golden honey
break the fast.

***

Shamayim: Heaven or sky

81

Reincarnation at the tag sale

on the empty beer-can-church-key table,
in the corner half hidden by Pat Patriot coasters
a Felix Mantilla baseball card from 1962–
JFK & I both were drawn to the stubby utility player.
Jack and Felix should never have gone to Texas.

a booth shelved with Care Bears and My Little Ponys,
fruit crates filled with curios on the dirt.
a tiny monkey knows about my crush on Jane Goodall.
he's carved from ebony except for two stone maze eyes–
his new digs, the pocket of my red plaid shirt.

hopping between displays, laughing girl carries
a metal rod with gimp lanyards hanging by their hooks.
my fingers were never nimble at Camp Samoset.
I couldn't finish a red and gold yard–
for a dollar and a smile, one is finally mine.

it's a bit of a shock to see a Chasidic vendor,
long grey beard, tzitzits, frum black hat.
his son, ginger pe'ot, reading Rashi, hands me
a wooden cube, Star of David carved top–
on Rosh Hashanah, a place to store my sins

An angel must be on my wing.
the Archie comic book where Midge dumps Moose,
stolen from my desk in third grade–
always suspected Randy Sussman.
good thing he lives in Detroit now

in the winter when I was a child,
we skied and swam at Eastover.
a quarter of the heated pool was outside.
the off-limits gift shop sold military models–
finally, a red cast iron Fokker triplane.

in my boyhood room under the one window,
a taupe radiator cover's drawer held treasures:
four rabbit foots, different furs, same clipped nails.
now, a yellow t-shirt, footless bunny with a frown–
"My name is Lucky", neon purple letters.

amid canteens, mess kits, Kabars, web gear, a
silver cigarette lighter, Marine logo, engraved:
To my Gunny hunny / Until we can light /
up together. Love, / Lily July 4 1943
–fifty dollars, a fair price

Hardy Boys' *While The Clock Ticked,* the cool book
read by popular boys (and Janet who wore jeans).
when my parents moved out of their house,
my complete set of the series, sent away–
thirty-eight years of regret end today.

junior high subjected me to shop class, Mr. Pitts
the guidance counselor laughed at my request, home-ec.
baking cookies– wrong, building bird houses–right.
the home-ec textbook fits sleekly under my arm–
girls were always nicer to me than boys.

Reclamation

weeping willow vines
harvested as whips by human spawn

who scale the broad bole,
reach for low branches

pull higher using forks as footholds,
poke feet above crowns,

nestle in the crotch's hollow
eighteen feet from lawn,

secreted in knotholes
books Beechies flashlights—

it's boys' retreat in dusk,
mothers call but the willow mutes

cocoon of beams in cave of bark,
pages turn   winds swoon

crickets' chirp from swamp,
sonata baring the soul

sons   pardoned for vines' plunder,
embraced by venerable boughs

In consideration of genius

Og drags antelope on branches over round rocks' back
corpse rolling in harmony creates a lucid track.

Haap, angry at mate's refusal to copulate
slams stones together, sparking fire to straw sack.

Blaise squaring triangles romantic with Pascalinex
probability of polygamy fruitful, slack.

Gottfried wagering odds/evens with rival Des Bosses
tyranny of theory binary seeding on/off hack.

Isaac under apple tree munching ripened mac
mockingbird shits, gravity vandalizing snack.

Ludwig packs ears exorcising distraction
prayer for silence culminates sonic lack.

Thomas sharpening quill to forge "all men equal"
Sally serves tea, rubbing shoulders with crafty knack.

Albert's space 'tween leg and stool spanning time, altering
relativity of smooth skin to bruised shin intact.

One small poet mangling words in ambiguity
ignites a genius for galling his wife to roar smack.

When the rain carries me home

our boots suction shin-high silt

the truck
      delayed by downpour dense as garden hoses flushing gnats
from a windshield
           bleats while backing
                      we shake slickers
              slap wading overalls
        it's a habit
    our union suits raise blisters
              socks knot saturated cotton

Gus draws a line of yellow ponchos
          levee to tailgate
      we pass sand bags
                        upstream trees crack and split
                pirouette from bank
          race to delta
        our rubber arms toss the next bag

a van honks
          limp salami sandwiches with cheese
    canteen bug juice

a roaring starts as a purr
                    hides in the river flow
          direction is wrong

Gus yells a warning
        irrigation ditch turns feral tributary
                  we spit mud
                      reach for roots
            currents lap waists
     Gus counts hoods
          Claire is missing
        NO she yells from the van

whitecaps ferry
        roof tiles
              porch door
                    vinyl siding
              cane rocker
    frayed overalls
        percale housecoat
              TV Guide
                    open parasol
              Moby Dick spine trailing pages
                    Hungryman meatloaf dinner

surface bubbles
        burps photographs
    French general pinning a medal on Gramp
              Gram in her Donut Dolly frock
    the couple dancing The Lindy
              Ma 'n Pa Dust Bowl babies
      Pa on Guadalcanal
Ma with a rivet gun

a boat collects us
        levees collapse
           we head south with the river
  away from flooded farms

away from the damned rain

The Scroll of Jerú

I am Jerú, daughter of Noah, the youngest child, matricidal bastard. My head crowns, molten core splaying mother's lava into a crust dogs lick until I am pink. The unicorn Dolf carries me in a goat sack hanging from his horn, nickers my cries into giggles. I suckle lions, grapple with apes.

My brothers, men with wives, wring my hair, curse its grease, spit on me. They squeal at my skin—flesh Father covets, oily, rare. When I begin to bleed, they strip me. Their stomachs jiggle, they pant, seep hemlock sweat. My nails engrave their necks, knuckles crack noses, knees knock gonads. The elder gnaws my ankle and pins me.

My brothers squabble, if neither can own me, they will split me or fight until one yields. Father decrees I marry and chooses a camel dealer who owes him three cows. The wedding contract will be sealed at Spring's first rain. I tell Father I want no man. Father is a pillar of sand.

In the morning, clouds whirlpool—red swallowing pink, purple engulfing red, until the sky is a maelstrom. *Silence. The Voice. The Command. The Covenant.*

Father and brothers build the ark. I climb trees to coax canaries, select lions I nursed with, choose cheetahs. My knees nestle Dolf's ribs, breasts slide astride his neck, lips whisper in his ears as hooves draw a map to lairs of mated pairs. Our final stop is Dolf's herd. He hangs his head, hammers his horn on the holy rock. I yank his mane, kiss the soft spot at the base of his horn, hum to a young mare. We tramp to the ark, clip clop the sole sound.

Lightning sears the desert. Deluge erupts from heaven. Father orders me to marry before boarding the ark, a loose maiden is sin. Dolf peers down from the deck. Water laps my ankles. I whistle. He leaps. We are wind as currents catapult the ark.

Dolf races up Mount Ararat, stands in the summit's waves. I trill, he whinnies. When the tide rises to our chins, the maelstrom forms an eye. *Silence. The Voice.* What now?

Two palms womb Dolf and me, fragrant fingers knead our flesh, launch us to sea. We thrash until finding our flippers and tail, then bob to the surface. Breathe, dive, click melodies. Our first Psalm is a mating call.

The seed of my human brothers covet the spot where I was stripped. There they wait for *The Voice* shed blood over *The Voice* fear *The Voice*. Dolf and I crest waves. *The Voice* whistles, we arc rainbows.

Cayo Costa

glistening path
        mother-of-pearl reflections
south to the shade of a mangrove point

woven white bone branches block the beach
chaos of angles, web carved by cetaceans
        baleen teeth spitting sand and sea

        erect trunks splay bleached boughs
lattice of limbs mocks in arrogant silhouettes
        gesturing to the currents

squall ripped roots
        buckle deadwood
into dismembered stalks

sand spurs carve mosaics
usher the invasion of caesar's weed
        harboring barbed spines

        seeds hid on sandals
swimsuit bottoms
        between the pads of paws

crawl through spiderwebbed
flowered stalks   emerge to
        arid breach in the canopy

an eagle perches at the rim of her treetop nest
        a flushed rice rat
loses the race with diving talons

In response to youthful Weltanschauung

I want to be a smiling old coot, fall asleep during phone calls.

I want to push a walker s l o w l y up the hallway, block young dudes bouncing wall-to-wall looking for a passing lane.

I want to drive 20 miles per hour in a 40-miles-per-hour zone, usher tailgating traffic.

I want to park my car at a 15-degree angle to the curb like Dad and Grandpa.

I want to lounge in a four-way adjustable recliner, seat rising to eject me when standing is too daunting a task.

I want to wear Coke-bottle glasses, corneas blue whale eyes.

I want to have a pill box with medication compartments for wake-up, after breakfast, before lunch, after lunch, before dinner, after dinner, bedtime.

I want to wear a bib, towel on my lap when I eat–spooning, chewing, and swallowing tax powers of concentration.

I want to see my sons marry, give me daughters-in-law to spoil.

I want my grandchildren to chauffeur me–I'll cluck at their music, chatter about seeing the Grateful Dead play *Dark Star* for 90 minutes one night in St. Louis when I was 19.

I want to celebrate the second iron anniversary.

I want to watch the president and her wife congratulate the first colonists on Mars.

I want to doze in my boudoir's hospital bed intrigued by what lies ahead, family all around reliving amusing moments while I drift from this world.

I want to be met in the next by family, friends–my dogs welcoming me home.

"The ghetto was not only a place of refuge for a persecuted minority but a great experiment in peace, in self-discipline and in humanism. As such it still exists and refuses to give up in spite of all the brutality that surrounds it. I was brought up among those people."
~ Isaac Bashevis Singer

On the nature of humor

       I'm on the gravy side.
Every day, a personal best.

Cancer could've killed me five years ago,
      but my chemo cocktail won.

My compadres and I in the infusion room,
              tethered to our pumps,
      pudding, wooden spoon,
   bottle after bottle of water,
crucial prognoses.

Some, like me, good odds.
      Others' cancer only held in check,
     perhaps 18 months,
         even three years.
Being short, they knew the sickest jokes.

I memorized them all.

Remotely Van Dyke

Mom's chin rests on my head, arms encircle mine
television flickers into worn canals of chair arms

my feet curl under her knees, heels nest against ottoman
blanket she slept under as a girl, drapes our legs

Mary burned the steaks for *Oh Rob!*'s client, Mom howls
I stare at her toes in a slipper peeking through moth holes

Rob mixes leftover Chicken Chow Mein with K-Rations
Mom cackles, I bridge my thighs, hold the fabric taut

the toes wink at me—better than not stepping on cracks,
counting in sevens, stepping floor tiles like a chess knight

cancer will leave Nana if I preserve this amulet
a hooded monk praying in the heart of a geode

Dick Van Dyke trips over the stool
Mom slips her feet off the ottoman

Mamele's hands

Tante Anna, Nana Edith's sister, dies in your arms—
    "You've been like a daughter to me."

Edith never learned to drive, relying on cousins for rides
    to bring chicken *zup* to a *foter* with the flu—
to hold a widow who outlived *kinder, bruders, shvesters*—
to relieve a *muter* of twins wearing dirty diapers—
before returning home to cook for family and 'company',
    drifters who otherwise slept outdoors.
Your bed—a rollaway in the kitchen next to the stove.

After closing Anna's eyes, you telephone her daughters,
    cousins who live a day's drive away—
rip your linen dress, cover mirrors, wash hands
    in cold water, bake for callers and mourners.

DRY

My eyes were dry when Zady Benny died.
In a coma on an ICU bed,
      hooked to ventilator, pic line,
      feeding tube, catheter.
Mom & I whispered, watching his face immobile.
Zady's eyes flickered, darted about the room,
      settled on my face. Tears flooded
      his cheeks. His lids closed.
We went home after a vigil,
      said Kaddish at sundown.

> *Old Country delicacies—calves foot jelly, intestines, spleen.*
> *Zady Benny-eight siblings share a straw bed, dirt floor.*
> *Ten year old boys work in fields. Girls, house servants.*

Last time I saw Grandpa Meyer alive, Thad & I
      drove Dad's car from Worcester to Revere.
Nana Ida made Thad tea, a plate.
I sat next to Grandpa's bed forcing questions,
      his face a yellow skinned skull.
The man who gave elegance to every word,
      rasped short answers.
He told me to leave, didn't want to be remembered
      infirm, jaundiced, skeletal, mute.
Thad & I dined at The Top Of The Pru.
Pretty pink filets, mashed potato sculptures, baby peas.
      I drank scotch neat after scotch neat after scotch neat.
Thad sat me down on the elevator floor,
      ferried me home.

> *The Tzars' bull conscripts smooth-faced scholar Shumuel.*
> *His sister Sisel hides in the shed, banished from sunlight.*

Dad's death, relieved sadness.
The last six weeks' agitation—kicking, moaning,
      navigating the cusp between worlds—
      lucid moments farther and farther spaced.

I last heard his voice from Paris. Incoherent mumbles
       settled into "I love you. I'm proud of you."
He drifted unresponsive. I made it to his bedside in time
       to kiss him, chant thanks, hold his cold hand.
He let go early the next morning.
Mom keened "What to do without him?"
I celebrated him in eulogy, shiva, silence as I shed sleep.
       Never with tears.

In the New Country, the great unwashed were free.
Free to work, free to trade their years for their children.
Tessie's twelve hour shifts end in the Shirtwaist factory blaze.

Dad's oldest brother Arnold died at fifty-six.
Three generations gathered for burial, black coats,
       black kippot, black mourners' siddurs.
We watched the coffin lower, gears creaking louder
       than seagulls.
Nana Ida stood into the wind, veil flapping, fingers
       clasped at her waist, mouth a flat line.
       We filled his crypt with dirt and rock, each
       shovelful a sickening hammer on pine.
Her eyes were dry.

During The Great Depression, pushing a fruit cart
meant there was food, overripe or bruised.

December 7, 1941—Nana Ida's birthday—
three sons eligible for 'service'.

The Old Country whispers—
camps, ovens, letters returned.

When I see someone sobbing, my arms hold them in a hug,
       I whisper "shhh… shhh…", lapels as handkerchiefs.
I am thanked for being sympathetic, compassionate, healing,
       my jealousy hidden like tears.

Rosh Hashanah 5775 – Yom Sheni

my mournful friend talks suicide
    i sleep crawling up a desert knoll
        an oasis drifts over the next dune
            gravel cuts the flesh between my toes
        wake to a spinning room–parched mouth
            twist my ankle getting off the bed
                stub a foot–throbbing nail bleeds
          we converse until throats are raw
        heads buried under the clay
i walk streets with earphones' music
        sidewalks my soles slapped for 60 years
          past the candy spa now a BBQ joint
            the mean pharmacy now a dry cleaner
        the kosher butcher now a pizza parlor
my sneakers find the house where I was born
        we lived on the first floor–Nana & Zady on the second
          porches look the same–and the driveway
            shouldn't it all seem smaller?
         two turns to the square that is a circle
    down the street without north in its name
cross a Little League field to the bleacher
        a Chasid in a black coat with cloth belt
          smiles–answers my *shanah tovah*
            his wife and toddler boy wave
        i turn my earphones off
        he asks me if i've heard the shofar today
i reply–*yesterday but not today*
    would I like to? yes–todah rabah
          the Chasid asks me to say the blessing
            i do without the proffered prayerbook
              he asks me to hold his Mahzor–
                so he can read the notes
              imagine he knows them by heart
          i did when i blew shofar at temple
        he slides out a squat black horn
     licks his lips–begins the calls
cycles once through the pattern

a second time for timbre
a third for his wife
he blows until exhausting his embouchure
asks me to walk with him—wife and son trailing—
through the park until our paths diverge
he is from new york—
a Yom Tov Chazzan at the yeshiva
have i ever been a Chazzan?
yes—over the summer while our rabbi is away
once during the winter
do i read torah?
yes—with Zady's Lithuanian-Latvian tones
old country trope—old during the great war
the trope interests him—would i chant a bit?
i cantillate the first aliyah of *Bereshith*
the parshah for the second day's service
he smiles—nods—thanks me
his colleague from Lithuania uses different notes
we exchange *gut yontifs*—he heading left me right
i turn music back on
follow the familiar path
past Zady's new house where i was a teen
to the new shul now 50 years old
find myself at my front door
it is a new year

***

Yom Sheni second day

Chasid Ultra-Orthodox Jew in this case Chabad-Lubavitch,
a Hasidic movement

shana tovah greeting for Rosh Hashanah, *Happy New Year* in Hebrew

shofar ancient trumpet made from a kosher ram's horn

todah rabah *Thank you very much* in Hebrew

Mahzor High Holiday Prayer Book (Rosh Hashanah & Yom Kippur)

yom tov literally "a good day", in meaning a High Holiday

chazzan cantor in a synagogue

trope from the Yiddish *trop*, ritual chanting notated by marks printed
in a bible

aliyah Torah *parshah*s are separated into these sections

Bereshith the first section of Genesis, Creation / "In The Beginning"

parshah the Old Testament is separated into these 52 weekly readings

gut yontifs holiday and Sabbath greeting, a Yiddish adaptation of
English & Hebrew – *gut* for "good", yontif for *Yom Tov* "good
day" – literally "good good day"

Tefillah shlosha
~ for Barbara Ann Barbato S.L.

In that moment—
          silence but not silent
                    seek out by looking in
                    search for a wispy spark
                    lit by the divine
          chameleon to the cornea
hidden by a yearning to be found

In that moment—
          waves never crashing
          fragile alignment of spirit—
                    cat chasing a pointer
                    rider posting a shifty horse
—to be in harmony is to let go
          surrender fear
become the other, be the self
          unhinged from compulsion
trust the current will lead
          never banishing breath

In that moment—
          calm in the heart of the gale
          close to what embraces me
before I am, after I am
living tied to the unfirm—
          spot of forest sunshine
          mountain pond warm spring
—stillness' acceleration
intimate with the unfathomable
          one with the unnamed

In that moment—
                    visions of anima
          words settle as chaff
     union with the sacred
willing release

About the Author

Richard H. Fox was born and bred in Worcester MA. He attended Webster University, as much artist colony as college, in the early 1970s. These diverse cultures shaped his world view and love of words. *Time Bomb*, his first collection of poetry, was published in 2013. He has been published in numerous journals and anthologies and was a Pushcart Prize nominee. A cancer survivor, he focuses many of his poems on treatment from the patient's point of view, drawing on hope, humor, and unforeseen gifts. Richard seconds Stanley Kunitz' motion that people in Worcester are "provoked to poetry."

Visit him at www.smallpoetatlarge.com.

Made in the USA
Charleston, SC
30 September 2015